THERE IS VIOLENCE AND THERE IS RIGHTEOUS VIOLENCE AND THERE IS DEATH, OR THE BORN-AGAIN CROW

THERE IS VIOLENCE AND THERE IS RIGHTEOUS VIOLENCE AND THERE IS DEATH, OR THE BORN-AGAIN CROW

CALEIGH CROW

PLAYWRIGHTS CANADA PRESS
TORONTO

Playwrights Canada Press
202-269 Richmond St. w., Toronto, ON M5V 1X1
416.703.0013 | info@playwrightscanada.com | www.playwrightscanada.com

LIBRARY AND ARCHIVES CANADA CATALOGUING IN PUBLICATION
Title: There is violence and there is righteous violence and there is death or, The born-again crow / Caleigh Crow.
Other titles: Born-again crow
Names: Crow, Caleigh, author.
Description: A play.
Identifiers: Canadiana (print) 20230509592 | Canadiana (ebook) 20230509630
   | ISBN 9780369104700 (softcover) | ISBN 9780369104717 (PDF)
   | ISBN 9780369104724 (EPUB)
Classification: LCC PS8605.R6885 T54 2023 | DDC C812/.6—dc23

Playwrights Canada Press staff work across Turtle Island, on Treaty 7, Treaty 13, and Treaty 20 territories, which are the current and ancestral homes of the Anishinaabe Nations (Ojibwe / Chippewa, Odawa, Potawatomi, Algonquin, Saulteaux, Nipissing, and Mississauga / Michi Saagiig), the Blackfoot Confederacy (Kainai, Piikani, and Siksika), néhiyaw, Sioux, Stoney Nakoda, Tsuut'ina, Wendat, and members of the Haudenosaunee Confederacy (Mohawk, Oneida, Onondaga, Cayuga, Seneca, and Tuscarora), as well as Metis and Inuit peoples. It always was and always will be Indigenous land.

We acknowledge the financial support of the Canada Council for the Arts, the Ontario Arts Council (OAC), Ontario Creates, the Government of Ontario, and the Government of Canada for our publishing activities.

For my mom.

Thank you for loving books so much,
loving plays so much, loving music so
much, and for loving life so much. I was
really lucky to be your daughter.

Miss you.

There is Violence and There is Righteous Violence and There is Death or, The Born-Again Crow was first produced by Thumbs Up Good Work Theatre, with the support of Calgary Arts Development, the Alberta Foundation for the Arts, and the Canada Council for the Arts, from March 1 to March 9, 2019, in the Motel Theatre in Arts Commons, Calgary, with the following cast and creative team:

Beth: Caleigh Crow
Crow: Colin Wolf
Mom: Deedra Salange Ladouceur
Tanner Braeden/Jane/Jim/Stephen: Noah Baker

Co-directors: Caleigh Crow and Colin Wolf
Live Music Composed and Performed by Sacha Crow
Stage Manager: Sara German
Set Design: Sydney Wolf
Properties: Sydney Wolf
Lighting Design: Kai Hall
Costume Design: Lindsey Kapitzke
Dramaturgy: Elena Eli Belyea

A NOTE ON THE SCORE

Without the score, it feels like half the play is missing. My ever-talented husband and creative partner, Sacha Crow, wrote an ambient, haunting score and performed it live in every show. This was the second time we collaborated on a theatre piece, and the first time we incorporated live music into our production.

Collaborating with Sacha has had an immense impact on my artistic practice. I firmly believe that a live theatre performance is a thousand times better when the music is also performed live. Liveness being the magic of our artform, it also resists archiving, especially in the form of a playtext.

If you'd like to produce this play, please prioritize a budget line for live music, and don't be afraid to play it loud.

CHARACTERS

Beth: A young woman. Metis or mixed Indigenous.
Crow: A talking crow.
Francine: Beth's mom. Metis or Indigenous.
Tanner Braeden: Beth's next-door neighbour and ex-boyfriend.
Jane: A news reporter.
Jim: President of the HOA.
Stephen: Beth's boss.

Cameraman: A cameraman for Jane.

A forward slash (/) indicates an interruption.

Italicized text in dialogue indicates overlapping speech.

SCENE 1

It is late in the day. Suburban backyard. There is a door to the house and a fence and trees. There is an assortment of outdoor furniture. There are garbage cans.

FRANCINE: I set everything up so you have a lot of space back here. It's all set up here. A lot of space and different areas—I thought you could sit here or you could sit over here, and maybe read, or whatever you'd like to do. I thought this could be a place you can come be in the sunshine and fresh air so I went ahead and set it all up for you.

BETH: Thanks, Mom.

FRANCINE: I thought it might be good for you to make a habit of filling these bird feeders I bought. You know, having something to keep track of, and someone who relies on you is a good way to learn—I just mean it's a good way to learn about life. I just think it will be good for you.

BETH: Right.

FRANCINE: And so what do you think?

BETH: It's nice, Mom.

FRANCINE: You'll sit out here sometimes?

BETH: Probably.

FRANCINE: Maybe this would be a good place for us to sit together.

BETH: Sure.

FRANCINE: You know I still can't stand television.

BETH: I know.

FRANCINE: Well I can't help it, I'm fussy and old, you know.

BETH: Yeah it's fine.

FRANCINE: I just prefer books.

BETH: Mom, I know. You don't have to watch TV. No one is gonna make you watch TV. And TV is doing fine without you anyway.

FRANCINE: I just prefer books.

    Beat.

And you know, we could sit out here together.

BETH: Yeah.

FRANCINE: Yeah.

BETH: I know you aren't saying you want to talk about what happened, but you do want to talk about it, and you don't want to say you want to sit out here and talk about it, but I know that you want to sit out here and talk about it.

FRANCINE: You're saying that, I'm not saying that.

BETH: I know what you mean, Mom, when you say you want to sit out here together. What else would we do but talk?

FRANCINE: I want to talk to you. Of course I want to talk to you. And I want to talk to you out here. But I didn't say I want to talk about what happened. You said that. My therapist said not to push you into talking about it so I'm not. I am going to let you tell me about it in your own time.

BETH: You talked to your therapist already?

FRANCINE: I called her on my way to pick you up.

BETH: Have you considered I never, ever want to talk to you about it?

FRANCINE: Never say never, Beth.

Beat.

My therapist also said that you might want to talk about it to someone else, and that I should support you in that. So if you want to invite a friend over to talk about it, then that's just fine with me.

Beat.

Do you remember Tanner Braeden? He's back for the summer.

Beat.

BETH: What else did your therapist say.

FRANCINE: About you?

BETH: About what happened.

FRANCINE: Nothing. No, I really don't know what happened. No one told me anything, none of the cops, not Stephen, no one really told me. I just picked you up like you asked me and now we're here. And that's all I know.

BETH: Well I certainly don't want to say anything about it today, right this second, since I just got here. And I'm still feeling a lot of feelings about it.

FRANCINE: Are they going to press charges?

BETH: So you do know. You know enough to know they're thinking of pressing charges. Where did you hear that? Where did you hear that? I haven't heard that. So where did you hear that?

FRANCINE: I just heard it around, I don't know.

BETH: Tell me everything you know and everything you've heard. This is not me talking about it this is me finding out exactly what you know and what you think I did. This will help me know what to say to you later if I do talk to you about it, so you had probably just tell me everything you've heard and everything you know.

FRANCINE: Alright. Alright. Sit down. Here's what I know. And it's really not a lot. I know you were working at the Superstore and there must have been something the matter with you. You went into work and worked half your shift, and then used a knife from the deli to fix a raw steak to Stephen's office door. Then you tried to drown your co-worker in a barrel of bulk rice flour. And then you knocked over a pyramid of soup cans. And then store security stopped you before you could start a fire in the magazines. I heard that Stephen wanted to press charges for wrecking up the store and causing a ruckus but that the cops calmed him down and you just had to pay him back for it. I heard Stephen fired you. And your co-worker was going to press charges because you attacked him. And I heard that Stephen wanted you to rebuild the soup can pyramid. But that's all I know.

BETH: So you know quite a bit.

FRANCINE: But that's all.

BETH: I'm not going to tell you how much of that is true.

FRANCINE: How long are you staying with me?

BETH: I don't know. But I like the bird feeders.

SCENE 2

One week later. Birds take off from the bird feeders as TANNER BRAEDEN *enters.*

TANNER BRAEDEN: Hey.

BETH: Hi.

TANNER BRAEDEN: Long time no see, right?

BETH: What are you doing here?

TANNER BRAEDEN: Hey, what's that about?

BETH: What do you want?

TANNER BRAEDEN: I just saw you over here and thought I'd come over and be nice to you.

BETH: Lie, lie, and lie. Three lies. How is that nice?

TANNER BRAEDEN: What?

BETH: You just saw me over here?

TANNER BRAEDEN: Yeah.

BETH: And you thought you'd come over.

TANNER BRAEDEN: Yeah.

BETH: And be nice.

TANNER BRAEDEN: Well, yeah.

BETH: My mom put you up to this.

TANNER BRAEDEN: She talked to my dad.

BETH: You can go then.

TANNER BRAEDEN: But maybe I actually like the plan and wanted to do it because I am actually nice.

Beat.

Hey, I'm not a kid anymore. Neither of us are kids anymore. I know I was an annoying brat. But I'm not a kid anymore and I know how to act better than I did.

BETH: I really don't need you feeling sorry for me.

TANNER BRAEDEN: I don't. I just thought you could use a friend.

BETH: I guess I'm not the type of person the neighbours will want to hang out with.

TANNER BRAEDEN: Yeah everyone here is fucking old. Or has like four kids.

BETH: Four kids and an infinite amount of neuroses around those kids.

TANNER BRAEDEN: A bunch of bubble boys and girls.

BETH: The opposite of you. You're like the opposite of a bubble boy.

TANNER BRAEDEN: What?

BETH: Bubble boys are encased, surrounded, and protected from the outside world. You aren't encased in anything. You're uncased. You're set loose.

TANNER BRAEDEN: Big time.

BETH: Usually if you're setting something loose it's like a wild animal. Or a hooligan or something. But you know it's not bad to have limits when you're growing up.

TANNER BRAEDEN: What are you talking about? What is good about limits?

BETH: That's how you get specific about something.

TANNER BRAEDEN: About what?

BETH: About who you are.

   Silence.

TANNER BRAEDEN: Let's get drunk.

BETH: Pass.

TANNER BRAEDEN: I know that's the only way I'll ever find out what you're doing here.

BETH: Nosy. And snoopy.

TANNER BRAEDEN: For what it's worth, I do know you. I've known you a long time. Even if we aren't really friends. I know what you're like anyway. I can see what you're like. And I know you're not easy to get along with. And I know things aren't easy for you. Generally.

BETH: Save it.

TANNER BRAEDEN: For another time? You got it.

> *TANNER BRAEDEN waves and leaves.* BETH *checks her feeders. She gets the bag of food and puts in a little more. She looks at the water in the bird bath. She looks up at the sky.*

SCENE 3

The next day. FRANCINE comes to the backyard.

FRANCINE: Nice day.

BETH: Mm-hm.

FRANCINE: How are the feeders?

BETH: I don't know. Seems to be working. There's less food in there than there was. I keep filling it up and there's lots of sparrows around. Lots of little chubby brown birds like that. And the crows too.

FRANCINE: That's good.

BETH: And I am reaping the benefits of being responsible for this bird feeder and soon I will be able to reintegrate into my natural habitat: wage slavery. It's all going according to plan.

FRANCINE: Hush.

BETH: How come you haven't asked me to leave or get a job?

FRANCINE: I don't exactly like living alone out here. It's not my favourite. It's been nice having you around again. Plus I don't really have a leg to stand on, do I? I don't have a job either.

BETH: That's not the same thing, really.

FRANCINE: I think people have always said I was a lazy no-job haver.

BETH: Why do people think having a job means you're a good person?

FRANCINE: It was the Protestants. Something about toiling for God.

BETH: Right. I don't think you're a lazy no-job haver.

FRANCINE: Thank you, Beth.

BETH: But moms are supposed to tell their kids to get jobs. Aren't you concerned about my productivity?

FRANCINE: I'm concerned.

BETH: But not about productivity.

FRANCINE: Sort of. I'm concerned that you aren't doing okay or that something happened to you.

BETH: And what makes you think that?

Pause.

I'm still not talking about that. I'm still not talking about it. But I will say that it wasn't my fault and I'm not the crazy one in this scenario.

FRANCINE: No one said you were crazy.

BETH: No one said to my face I'm crazy but they fired me for being crazy, even though no one said to my face that I'm crazy.

FRANCINE: They fired you because you were threatening people, frightening customers, and fire-starting.

BETH: Some people deserve to be threatened and some people should know what it feels like to be frightened! I can't stand it! I can't stand it! It is so obvious that they've never ever been frightened in their life.

FRANCINE: You're making assumptions and judgments.

BETH: Yeah and I'm the first and only person to ever do so.

FRANCINE: Well you showed them all didn't you?

BETH: I don't get who I'm supposed to be about everything. Why should anyone care about the Superstore?

FRANCINE: The Superstore cares what happens to the Superstore. Your boss cares if you destroy the store. And that's why they fired you.

BETH: That is not why they fired me. / They did not fire me for that. It was very convenient for them that I did all those things but that is not why they fired me.

FRANCINE: You have to be responsible for your actions.

BETH: I would do all that again in a heartbeat. I am more than responsible for my actions. I love my actions. I am madly in love with my actions.

FRANCINE: / Beth, don't say that.

BETH: It's true. I wish I was able to burn that Superstore / to the ground.

FRANCINE: Beth, stop it.

BETH: Everything in it. The bakery deserves to burn, the deli, the cereal aisle, the fruit, the coconut milk section, the lady razors section, the healthy candy section, the pills section, the whole damn place. Everything.

FRANCINE: *But there were innocent people in that store that could have been hurt. You scared them all pretty good, and your co-workers too. Well the people in the store were—*

BETH: *Some people deserve to be threatened and some people should know what it feels like to be frightened! I can't stand it! I can't stand it! It is so obvious that they've never ever been frightened in their life. Who did I hurt?*

What, hurt? Were they hurt? Did I hurt them?

FRANCINE: Well, no but—

BETH: Then I don't see why I'm labelled as the psycho who can't keep a job! And now I'm the psycho who lives with her retarded mother!

FRANCINE: Beth!

> *Pause. FRANCINE goes inside. After a while, BETH fills up the bird feeder. She sits back down.*

BETH: Everything is fucked. Everything. Everything, everything.

The CROW flies in for the first time. He drops off something shiny into the feeder.

What was that? Did you drop something?

CROW: Yes.

BETH: You talked?

CROW: Yes.

BETH: What else can you say?

CROW: I can say anything you can say.

They consider each other.

BETH: Say something else.

CROW: Like what?

BETH: What do you want?

CROW: Just to say thank you. You're really nice to the birds back here.

BETH: My mom set out the feeders, I just put the food in them.

CROW: Thank you for that.

BETH: I'm not really sure how to deal with this.

(calls out) Mom? Can you come out here?

FRANCINE: What?

BETH: Do you see that crow right there?

FRANCINE: Yes.

BETH: Hello? Hello?

FRANCINE: I'm not happy with you right now.

BETH: Yes but listen: hello?

FRANCINE: Are you going to apologize?

BETH: Yes, I will. I promise. But that crow was just talking.

FRANCINE: Like squawking?

BETH: No, it was talking. It was speaking English.

    Pause.

FRANCINE: What did it say?

BETH: It said thanks for the food.

FRANCINE: I saw that video on YouTube of the crow that said the F-word. Did you see that one?

BETH: Yes I saw the video of the crow that said the F-word.

FRANCINE: Birds can learn to mimic all sorts of sounds.

BETH: Right. But do you think it could learn to talk? Like we talk?

FRANCINE: What do you mean?

BETH: Is it possible that a crow could learn to have a thoughtful conversation?

FRANCINE: No.

BETH: I thought nature was miraculous.

FRANCINE: No, God is miraculous.

BETH: But miracles, miracles happen?

FRANCINE: Miracles happen. You're my miracle. Which is why it hurt my feelings when you—

BETH: Not now. Do you think a crow could learn to talk?

FRANCINE: No, I don't see how.

BETH: Do you think that crow could learn to talk?

FRANCINE: Beth.

BETH: What about Koko the gorilla?

FRANCINE: I read on the internet somewhere that gorilla was a faker.

BETH: A faker?

FRANCINE: It was all really exaggerated. Like, yes, she could use sign language, *kind of*. But the extent to which she could use sentences and grammar and stuff was all really exaggerated.

BETH: You think Koko the gorilla is fake?

FRANCINE: I just saw something on the internet about it, that it was all really exaggerated. But what does that have to do with this crow?

BETH: I'm just wondering if it's possible for this crow to learn to speak either as a miracle by God or by extensive language studies, possibly under the guidance of an English-speaking human.

FRANCINE: I don't think so. But maybe the crow did say something to you. There's the crow that said the F-word, and they make all kinds of sounds that they hear, like city noises they're getting really good at. Maybe you could teach this one something. But not the F-word please, first of all it's been done. Secondly it doesn't seem right because the crow won't know he's being rude.

BETH: Hey look at this. He dropped this on the feeder.

FRANCINE: Let me see. Let me see it up close. Well I don't know. It likes you, I guess. I didn't know—I never heard of anything like that.

BETH: I can't believe it.

FRANCINE: Well you're doing a wonderful thing feeding these crows! You're welcome! Come on, Beth, say you're welcome.

BETH: Mom.

FRANCINE: Here, we'll find a special place for you to put it.

BETH: I wanna stay and watch 'em eat.

FRANCINE: Okay. I'm making supper.

BETH: Okay.

FRANCINE: Anything else you want to say?

BETH: Mom, I'm sorry. I shouldn't have said that. I don't know why I said that, it was horrible.

FRANCINE: That really hurt my feelings.

BETH: I know. It was totally uncalled for.

FRANCINE: People actually called me that, you know, growing up. So it really hurt when you said that because you're the person who knows me best in this whole wide world.

BETH: You can't protect me from everything, even from my own mistakes. But I don't have to take it out on you.

FRANCINE: I want you to be independent. But I might know some things that you don't know, since I am older than you. Much older, these days.

BETH: Mom, you are aging at the same rate as everybody else.

FRANCINE: Now say I look amazing for my age.

BETH: You look amazing. You are amazing. Can you forgive me?

FRANCINE: Yes. But you owe me the biggest favour ever.

BETH: Of course, anything to make it up to you. What do you want?

FRANCINE: I'll think of something.

FRANCINE goes inside. BETH watches the CROW a little bit.

BETH: Hello?

CROW: Hello.

BETH: Okay so you only talk to me?

CROW: Yes.

BETH: I guess I can live with that. How can you talk? Can all the crows talk?

CROW: I'm the only one that talks to you.

BETH: Are you a special crow?

CROW: Yes I'm a special crow.

BETH: I'm afraid.

CROW: I know.

BETH: But I feel strong.

CROW: That's why I'm here.

BETH: Really. That actually makes perfect sense to me.

CROW: What happened at the Superstore?

BETH: I'm still not talking about that.

CROW: You have to. You have to talk about it. You keep dancing around the topic. A very cheap way to keep us in suspense.

BETH: How do you know anything about it?

CROW: I'm a talking crow.

BETH: I don't trust you. What happened at the Superstore was really bad.

CROW: But here you are.

BETH: I'm not talking about it.

CROW: You are constantly talking about it.

BETH: I'm afraid.

CROW: I know. I want to be your friend, Beth.

BETH: Why?

CROW: Listen. I'm special and you're special too.

BETH: My mom says nature's very important. You're part of nature so you should be important to me. What else can you do? Just talk? Or are you magic in other ways?

CROW: It wasn't easy for me to learn. I had to teach myself. I never wanted to learn, until one day a spirit told me I could. So I wanted to learn to impress the spirit. And become the spirit.

BETH: What spirit?

CROW: Not what spirit—who spirit. All of them. The one inside me. My own spirit. Everyone else's. And your spirit. There's not an end to spirits. I can't nail down exactly who the spirit is. The spirit of all things—do you know it?

BETH: I think so—is it God?

CROW: I don't know. I don't know. That might be the wrong question.

BETH: But in paintings of saints—do they have it?

CROW: What's a painting?

BETH: Do you really not know what a painting is?

CROW: What's a saint?

BETH: How does— How do you know what a spirit is but not what a painting of a saint is.

CROW: Where would I have seen one? Where do I go to see one? Or how would I find out?

BETH: I guess you've only really been outside. Is that right?

CROW: That's right.

BETH: So this is a miracle right? A miracle of nature?

CROW: Do you believe in miracles, Beth?

BETH: I guess I might. This feels normal. I think you have me under a spell. So I don't freak out and scream.

CROW: Seems that way. But maybe not.

BETH: My mom's therapist says I shouldn't call myself insane. So I'm not saying I'm insane right now. Even though I really am not sure. At all. About what's going on here. Did you bring me this piece of glass?

CROW: Yes.

BETH: What for?

CROW: Don't you like it?

BETH: Yeah I really do. I really like it.

CROW: That's why.

SCENE 4

The next morning. BETH *brings out the food. She finds the* CROW *and one other crow.*

BETH: Oh! Another one! A friend of yours.

CROW: You give me enough food that I can share. Is it okay if I bring hungry birds here? Will you run out?

BETH: Maybe I'll ask my mom.

CROW: What do you think she'll say?

BETH: I think she'll say that this is very meaningful. She likes things to be meaningful and I think this is something like what she would want.

CROW: Then do you really need to ask her?

BETH: If it's just a few more she probably won't even notice. She'll probably say—that's the order of things. That's the way it should be. I'm helping those in need.

CROW: You pay very close attention to what she says.

BETH: She's always talking. I listen really hard because she hides what she's really trying to say behind other things, things that don't mean as much. So you have to really listen. That's the way to understand her. Otherwise it all sounds like nonsense.

CROW: But she's always talking.

BETH: Yes she never stops really, even if no one asks her anything she talks. Even if there's no one else there, she talks to herself all the time.

CROW: What does she say when she's alone?

BETH: I can't always tell. She mutters, you know? But she's had a hard life so she's allowed to mutter around the house. And she's entitled to her privacy about it.

CROW: Bad things?

BETH: No. No, not bad things. She's good, she's a good person. You know just cause you're here with me doesn't mean you get to know everything about me. Or my mom. Why are you asking me anyway?

CROW: I'm sorry, Beth. I want to get to know you better. That's all. Thank you for the food. My friend thanks you too. I brought this for you.

He reveals a dangly earring.

BETH: It's very beautiful, thank you. I'll put it away somewhere safe. Thank you.

CROW: Are you alone out here?

BETH: Yes.

CROW: Were you alone out there too?

BETH: Yes.

CROW: People don't understand you.

BETH: I guess not.

CROW: It's not your fault.

BETH: Maybe it is, though. Maybe everything that's ever made me cry is my own fault. Because I didn't get strong enough, or I didn't make the right choice at the most important time. I should have done everything different.

CROW: Can you change everything?

BETH: No.

CROW: Can you change anything?

BETH: I don't know. I hate thinking it's not fair. I feel like a whiny brat when I think it's not fair. And I never, ever want to be a whiny brat. But I look around me and it seems like everyone else has this clear, straight road in front of them, and every choice is the right one. No one else acts how I do. It seems like those other kind of people always get what they want. And the only reason I don't have what I want is because I'm stupid, irresponsible, and I make the exact wrong choice. So it's my own fault.

CROW: You don't really believe it's your own fault.

BETH: But isn't it all up to me? Who else is going to make the right choice for me?

CROW: Maybe you don't make all your choices. Maybe there is a road. Maybe it's all laid out.

BETH: Then why don't I have a stable, normal life? Wouldn't I have one if I really wanted one?

CROW: I don't have a normal life.

BETH: You could be a demon for all I know.

CROW: So what?

BETH: Demons are evil.

CROW: You've seen evil before, right?

BETH: I have.

CROW: And what happened to that evil?

BETH: Nothing.

CROW: So, people get away with things. Why can't you get away with things?

BETH: I'm easy to punish, I guess. I'm just a grocery store clerk. I don't even have healthcare.

    Beat.

You can bring as many hungry crows here as you like. I'll put out more food. I'll put out more feeders. As many as you like.

CROW: Thanks. You must realize you don't control everything in the universe. Yet.

SCENE 5

Three days later. More and more crows come. There are about twenty crows now. As BETH's putting some food out TANNER BRAEDEN enters. CROW flies off.

TANNER BRAEDEN: Hey Beth.

BETH: Hey.

TANNER BRAEDEN: What are you up to?

BETH: I'm feeding my crows.

TANNER BRAEDEN: I heard about your crows. They come into our yard all the time too. They shit everywhere. My dad says they're pests but my mom thinks it's nice, you feeding all these birds.

BETH: Okay thank you for telling me all that, I didn't ask you but thank you anyway.

TANNER BRAEDEN: I wanted to see all the crows myself but they flew off I guess. Hey you wanna see what I got for my birthday?

TANNER BRAEDEN shows BETH his rifle.

BETH: That looks awful.

TANNER BRAEDEN: It's fun.

BETH: What do you shoot at?

TANNER BRAEDEN: Cans and stuff when my mom's around. But my dad and I shoot at squirrels and birds.

BETH: Birds?

TANNER BRAEDEN: My dad says if I practice shooting at moving targets I'll get better faster.

BETH: Practice for what?

TANNER BRAEDEN: I don't know, Beth, but it's good to have a diverse skill set. That's what my dad says. Here grab some pop cans I'll show you how it works.

BETH: I watch TV, I know how guns work.

TANNER BRAEDEN: Don't you wanna watch me shoot?

BETH: You are interrupting my whole day.

BETH gets some cans out of the recycling bin.

TANNER BRAEDEN: *(teasing)* Look Beth, I know you have to spend your days feeding rats and pigeons or whatever but look, I have a nice shiny new toy and I want to share it with you. Get like, four or five cans. Guns are cool, Beth. You've never seen a shoot-em-up? Really?

Further over. No, the other way. You know what your problem is, Beth? You're noble. Everyone who was ever called noble in a book or a movie has acted just like how you act. You'd probably have a lot more fun if you weren't so noble.

BETH: Can you shoot the cans now please?

TANNER BRAEDEN: Well you gotta get out of the way! I don't wanna accidentally hit you.

BETH: So is your aim just like not good then or—

TANNER BRAEDEN: —Will you shut up, Beth, and get out of the way? It's just safety.

> *BETH moves out of the way.*

> *TANNER BRAEDEN aims and fires.*

WHOO! See? This is fucking awesome!

BETH: Mhm.

TANNER BRAEDEN: I'm James Bond!

> *He fires.*

BETH: You're so full of shit.

TANNER BRAEDEN: Don't be such a bitch.

BETH: Fuck you.

He fires.

TANNER BRAEDEN: Beth, I didn't mean it like BITCH, I was kidding, I meant it like, you know, don't be such—

BETH: —such a bitch. I heard you.

TANNER BRAEDEN: Wow, you really can't take a joke can you? You never call your friends bitches as like a joke, or like, you never say, as a joke to your friends "you're such an asshole"?

BETH: You're such an asshole.

TANNER BRAEDEN: I guess you don't have any friends anyway.

He fires.

BETH: You shouldn't be shooting at birds. If I catch you doing something like that I'm going to—

TANNER BRAEDEN: You're going to what, Beth? You're gonna get mad? You're gonna yell at me? Are you gonna hit me? I've got a gun, Beth. You're not really in any position to be threatening me. I should be threatening you! You're being really annoying when I'm just trying to have some fun shooting pop cans.

BETH: And birds.

TANNER BRAEDEN: Christ, Beth! Don't act like you're better than me. I heard about what you did at the Superstore. Do you wanna try the gun or not?

BETH takes the gun and shoots at the cans.

Violence is human nature. We've been killing each other all over the world since forever. It's just always been that way. Every society has fighters that protect the weak. Don't you have sacred warriors in your culture? And they're the ones that get to wear the headdresses right? See, every culture honours protectors. That's what my dad says. That's why I should have this valuable skill set, like I said before, because I might have to protect myself and my family.

BETH: Do you just repeat everything your dad says?

TANNER BRAEDEN: At least I have a dad to teach me this stuff.

Beat.

Sorry. That was shitty. I know your dad—

BETH: Died.

TANNER BRAEDEN: Yeah, well, I'm sorry. I just meant, that, like. I don't know, maybe there's stuff you don't know and I could help you. That's really all I want. Anyway now you know how to shoot a gun.

She hands him over the rifle.

BETH: I'm bored now. Maybe you better go.

TANNER BRAEDEN: Look Beth, with everything going on with you, you need someone. You need someone to protect you. Otherwise everything will just stay fucked up for you.

TANNER BRAEDEN exits.

SCENE 6

*Three days later. More crows come. FRANCINE calls the news.
JANE, the reporter, arrives with a CAMERAMAN. BETH shows the
reporter her set-up. JANE takes notes and pictures.*

JANE: Wow, Beth, quite the set-up you've got here. Nice yard. How
long have you been doing this?

BETH: About two weeks.

JANE: Two weeks? That's not very long.

BETH: Word travels fast, I guess.

JANE: So we're just going to set up here and I'm going to ask you a
few questions. It's a very charming little story.

Okay, so, what do you feed them?

BETH: I fill this part here with peanuts. They like the ones with the
shell on better. So you put them all here and then I get the dog food
and put that all in the grass.

JANE: Dog food?

BETH: My mom read about a scientist who says that crows can really
benefit from dog food and they keep eating it all so they must really like it.

JANE: And where do they leave you your gifts?

BETH: They leave them right here in this tray where the food goes.

JANE: And what sorts of things do they give you?

BETH: Little bits of things, bits of glass and buttons. People lose a lot of earrings I guess because they bring a lot of earrings. And beads.

JANE: Do you keep everything they give you?

BETH: Yes, right here in this tackle box.

JANE: How many crows come here?

BETH: There's probably at least fifty that come here now. Plus all the other birds.

JANE: That's a lot of crows!

BETH: Yes it is.

JANE: I was talking to your neighbours, they think that's a lot of crows too. They were saying it might be too many. What do you think about that?

BETH: Those people don't know what they are talking about.

JANE: No?

BETH: No.

JANE: No?

BETH: No.

JANE: Jim Abernathy thinks it might be too many.

BETH: Why did you talk to Jim?

JANE: What do you think about that?

BETH: I don't. He doesn't understand what I'm doing here, what I'm accomplishing.

JANE: What are you accomplishing?

BETH: I'm changing this place. I'm changing it back. I'm reminding all these rich people who this place really belongs to.

JANE: And who is that? The homeowners' association?

BETH: The HOA can choke.

JANE: They don't like what you're doing here, do they?

BETH: I'd rather the birds like me. And they do.

JANE: Will you show me a few of your favourites from your collection?

BETH: I like this one, but it has to stay in the container.

JANE: What is it? A screw?

BETH: A very rusty screw. If I let you touch it and you got tetanus the neighbourhood would freak out and make me stop.

JANE: How do you know that?

BETH: They've been calling my mom and sending us letters and stuff. It doesn't matter. It's a free country, isn't it?

JANE: Why do you like this screw?

BETH: You don't see a crow carrying around a screw that much. Maybe it was trying to build its house.

JANE: Right. That's a good reason.

BETH: Yeah, it's a real standout. Here's one, second favourite. It says "best." I wonder all the time where the other half is.

JANE: And which one is first favourite?

BETH: This one.

JANE: How come?

BETH: It was the first thing he ever brought me. Well, I mean. It was the first one they ever brought to me.

JANE: Well, I've got all I need here, are you ready to go live?

BETH: Live?

CAMERAMAN starts setting up for a live broadcast. JANE checks her hair and makeup.

JANE: Yes, I'm going to go live on Facebook for the station. I'll just do a quick intro and then ask you a few questions like the ones I just asked you. Then I'll sign off and that's it! 'Kay?

BETH: Okay . . .

JANE: Okay, great. Alright, I'll just set this up here. Okay.

(to CAMERAMAN) Is this crooked? Okay, got it.

> *CAMERAMAN gives a thumbs up. BETH stands awkwardly to the side.*

Hey, Facebook! It's Jane Lafontaine coming to you with another KPPFJ Facebook New Minute Break, live on the KPPFJ Facebook page. I want to know: do we have any bird fans following us today? Today's story is for you guys! I'm here in the suburban community of Chestwood where a mother and daughter have set up a remarkable refuge for crows. Every day they put out food for the neighbourhood crows and the crows show their gratitude by bringing gifts for the pair. That's right, these crows have been leaving behind small items in the very same feeders they eat from! But here's where this story takes a confrontational turn. The sheer amount of food the two neighbourhood eccentrics put out for these crows attracts such a vast number that they are terrorizing the neighbourhood. Jim Abernathy has said that his small children have been frightened daily and that his car is covered in excrement. He is planning to take action by lodging a complaint with city officials. I'm here with Beth, one of the crow people. Hi Beth, say hello to Facebook.

BETH: Hello everyone.

JANE: So you told me you have about fifty crows that visit you, is that correct?

BETH: Yes.

JANE: And where do they sleep?

BETH: Pardon me?

JANE: Where do all these crows sleep?

BETH: Um, I don't know.

JANE: They've been taking shelter in all the trees surrounding the cul-de-sac, and in some of the roofs of your neighbours.

BETH: Oh, okay, well—

JANE: Are you concerned at all that your pet project might be damaging other people's homes?

BETH: I'm concerned. But I don't want to stop. This is a good thing.

JANE: For you?

BETH: For the crows. For the neighbourhood too. It's important not to neglect nature. Can we stop?

JANE: We're live, Beth.

BETH: You said you were going to ask the same questions. Are you going to ask about my collection?

JANE: Of course. Beth keeps her collection in a quaint tackle box, and she's even gone through the trouble to rank and label them. Isn't that adorable?

BETH: Thanks.

JANE: Show us this one?

BETH: I can't take it out of there, remember?

JANE: Tell the Facebook viewers what it is.

BETH: It's a rusty screw.

JANE: How macabre!

BETH: I think it's kind of cool.

JANE: And tell everybody what you feed them.

BETH: I feed them a few different things, a lot of peanuts and they love dog food.

JANE: Crows that love dog food!

BETH: Yeah, it's pretty unexpected.

JANE: Well thank you, Beth. That's about all the time that we have. Thanks to everyone for tuning into another KPPFJ Facebook News Minute Break with me, Jane Lafontaine. Hope to see you all next time and remember to hit like on this video and comment below if you have ever had a pet bird. You can also follow us on Instagram

@KPPFJNewsStation (all one word) and you can follow my
personal account, @RealJLafontaine. See you next time for another
KPPFJ Facebook News Minute, I'm Jane Lafontaine, signing off.

*CAMERAMAN gives another thumbs up and starts taking down
his equipment.*

Thanks for doing this again, Beth. Quite the set-up you got here.

BETH: No problem, thank you.

JANE: Hey, let me know if this story develops, this is something I
think will be really interesting to our viewers and might even make
the nightly broadcast.

BETH: Really?

JANE: Yeah, people love neighbourhood gossip. It's just such a
real story you know, it's really good for starting conversations and
generating content. And likes.

BETH: That's good, I guess.

JANE: Well, that's it for me, I can just show myself through the house
so I can thank your mother again too. Have a great day! Enjoy the
birds!

JANE and CAMERAMAN exit.

BETH: Thanks, you too! Have a great day, I mean, not about the birds.

BETH puts away her tackle box and takes out her phone.

FRANCINE enters.

FRANCINE: She's nice. How did that go?

BETH: Terrible.

FRANCINE: She just said it was great!

BETH: Great for her maybe. But I think I came off like a total freak.

FRANCINE: No I'm sure it was fine!

BETH: I'm trying to find it now.

FRANCINE: It just happened.

BETH: It was live.

FRANCINE: On TV?

BETH: On Facebook.

FRANCINE: Okay. Interesting.

FRANCINE pulls out her phone.

BETH: Shit!

FRANCINE: Did you find it?

BETH: No not yet, but I have a notification from one of my fucking co-workers. Ex co-workers. Shit! What a fucking bitch! Fuck you!

FRANCINE: What? What?

BETH: She just linked to the story and posted "this was my co-worker who freaked out and went pyro AF in my department and got fired lol Looks like she's much better off without the Superstore laughing crying emoji four times"!! She tagged me in it! She didn't just write my name she tagged me!

FRANCINE: Uh oh.

BETH: Yeah, big fucking uh oh. Fuck!

> *BETH discards her phone.*

FRANCINE: It's okay.

BETH: This is so embarrassing. I hate this shit.

FRANCINE: Hey, it'll be okay. It doesn't matter what other people think.

BETH: It does, actually, if I ever want to get a job I need people to think I'm not a bird girl or whatever.

FRANCINE: But you are a bird girl. Come inside and I'll find some cookies. I think there's cookies in there. Let's watch *Chopped*.

> *FRANCINE and BETH exit.*

SCENE 7

TANNER BRAEDEN comes over with wine the next night.

TANNER BRAEDEN: Hey loser.

BETH: Shut up.

TANNER BRAEDEN: What are you doing?

BETH: Reading. Listening to music.

TANNER BRAEDEN: Wanna hang out or something?

   Beat.

I was bored so I thought I'd see what you're doing. Turns out you're doing nothing too.

BETH: I'm reading. And listening to music.

TANNER BRAEDEN: Yeah that's what I said. Nothing. I brought wine.

BETH: No thanks.

TANNER BRAEDEN: Just a glass.

Pause.

BETH: Okay.

TANNER BRAEDEN: What are you listening to?

BETH: Radiohead. What?

TANNER BRAEDEN: Nothing. Just kinda . . . Gen X of you. Do you like being depressed?

BETH: Is that what listening to Radiohead means?

TANNER BRAEDEN: Yes.

BETH: Well, we have a real problem in our society then 'cause Radiohead is like one of the biggest bands ever. Like they've sold thousands and thousands of records. Thousands. And thousands. Hundreds of thousands.

TANNER BRAEDEN: I dunno I just never got into them I guess.

BETH: Okay.

TANNER BRAEDEN: I mean, the guy admits to being a creep.

BETH: So you just like. Don't get it. Like you just don't get the song or the lyrics . . .

TANNER BRAEDEN: I guess not. We're pretty different. You and me, I mean.

BETH: Yeah.

TANNER BRAEDEN: I guess we've always been pretty different even when we were kids.

BETH: Yeah.

TANNER BRAEDEN: Well, you're different. You're like nobody else I ever knew.

BETH: Saying stuff like that to me is why I'm so arrogant.

TANNER BRAEDEN: I don't think you're arrogant. Maybe a little. But I like that about you. I get you. So why'd you do it?

BETH: Do what?

TANNER BRAEDEN: The thing at the Superstore.

BETH: Christ.

TANNER BRAEDEN: Well?

BETH: Seemed like the right thing to do at the time. It was the most purely selfish thing I've ever done.

TANNER BRAEDEN: Everybody is selfish sometimes. It's human nature.

BETH: Having a psychotic break in the grocery store as therapy is human nature?

TANNER BRAEDEN: No one is perfect. I've made messed up decisions and messed up my life. I'll probably do that a few times before it's all over.

BETH: I think you're supposed to try not to, though.

TANNER BRAEDEN: Nobody's perfect.

BETH: But I think you're supposed to try.

TANNER BRAEDEN: But since everyone messes up I think you're supposed to like, forgive people and shit. You know, eventually people will move on with their lives. You will too. They'll move on from the KPPFJ Facebook Minute too.

BETH: No! You saw that?

TANNER BRAEDEN: I did, I did. I liked it. I've never seen you properly bewildered before.

BETH: Shut up.

TANNER BRAEDEN: It's true! It was cute.

BETH: She was supposed to just ask me about the collection and then she starts going off about Jim and like, trying to make me feel guilty or something.

TANNER BRAEDEN: I guess that's what the real story is though, because of the tension. And conflict and drama.

BETH: It's so stupid.

TANNER BRAEDEN: No it's not. You came off as more endearing than anything else, at least to me. You genuinely care about these birds. And that's infectious, you know? Eventually the neighbours will just get used to it and back off. Even though it is like, a lot of crows. Does it ever get noisy?

BETH: Yes. And they pick the weirdest times to be loud.

TANNER BRAEDEN: Don't worry. It will all turn out. Let's hear some Radiohead.

> *She gives him an earbud. He teases her a bit by dancing sarcastically. Then they start dancing to it more like, for real.*

Remember when you got your wisdom teeth taken out, and we went for ice cream, and you were still woozy from the painkillers? They were playing a song, something like this, something moody. And you said you loved the song so much. So much you could dance right there. But you couldn't really move because you were so out of it, so you started sort of half-swaying in the Dairy Queen, with a big puffy face holding a banana split.

BETH: It's hazy but I do.

TANNER BRAEDEN: I remember.

BETH: I also remember you stealing some of those painkillers to sell to your cousin.

TANNER BRAEDEN: I wanted him to think I was cool! I remember all of that. I remember our first kiss—

BETH: Tanner, don't.

TANNER BRAEDEN: Beth! Beth, don't be like that.

BETH: What did you come over here for?

TANNER BRAEDEN: Look, we've been hanging out a lot and I still like you. I still like you, Beth! I can't help it. I like you. I like you. And we were just teenagers before. You're so excitingly different than before and you're so the same as you've ever been. And I still like you.

BETH: Can we just leave that alone please?

TANNER BRAEDEN: I tried but I can't! I can't stop thinking about it.

BETH: What is there to think about?

TANNER BRAEDEN: Just that you know, I regret what happened.

BETH: You regret that.

TANNER BRAEDEN: Yeah, well, I've been thinking that I'm sorry about all that.

BETH: You're thinking that you're sorry? You've been thinking about how you're sorry?

TANNER BRAEDEN: Don't say that like it's insane.

BETH: It is insane! There's no reason to rehash all that, which is exactly why I haven't.

TANNER BRAEDEN: Well that's what I've been thinking.

BETH: Just to be clear, thinking about how you're sorry is not the same thing as actually saying you're sorry.

TANNER BRAEDEN: I just think that there's a reason it didn't work out then and that it's pretty cosmic / that we're next-door neighbours again after all your troubles and like that you know, maybe now is the right time. Yeah, cosmic.

BETH: / Cosmic?!

It absolutely is not the right time. You are trouble with a capital T.

TANNER BRAEDEN: You like trouble.

BETH: That is not cute, at all.

TANNER BRAEDEN: I don't get why you hate me so much.

BETH: I don't hate you! I just don't want to fuck you because you're bored.

TANNER BRAEDEN: I'm supposed to just sit here and let you say all this stuff to me like you know what I'm thinking? You are actually capable of hurting people, Beth.

BETH: I know that.

TANNER BRAEDEN: So you know, I am sorry for my part in what happened. I'm sorry for it. I'm sorry.

BETH: Do you think I'm stupid? Did you think you could come here and with all this talk about forgiveness and forgiving myself for what happened at the Superstore that I'd naturally want to forgive you for what you did? Did you think you could come here and say all that, then what? We fuck?

TANNER BRAEDEN: I'm just telling you how I feel.

BETH: Well you told me and I told you to drop it.

TANNER BRAEDEN: Beth, please just listen to me, and just think about what—

FRANCINE enters with laundry for the clothesline.

FRANCINE: Hey, you two. What's new?

TANNER BRAEDEN: Uh, nothing much. Just hanging out. Listening to Radiohead.

FRANCINE: Beth's trying to convert you, eh?

TANNER BRAEDEN: Yeah, she's trying. But I just don't know if she thinks I'm the right sort of person to listen to Radiohead.

FRANCINE: You mean not depressed? Ha!

TANNER BRAEDEN: Yeah, that's what I said.

FRANCINE: She's always trying to turn me onto some new kind of music.

BETH: I'm not trying to convert anybody. It doesn't hurt to try something new.

FRANCINE: Of course, I'm just too old for that sort of thing. Although even when I was your age I was saying the same thing. I'm just too fussy I guess, I like the same things I've always liked.

Weird silence.

Oh jeez, I've interrupted, haven't I?

BETH & TANNER BRAEDEN: No.

FRANCINE: Well I'll be out of your hair in a minute, just let me hang this stuff.

TANNER BRAEDEN: That's a pretty old-school method.

FRANCINE: Well, what I have I been saying? I'm old-school. Or just old. Ha!

> *FRANCINE hangs all the laundry even if it takes a weirdly long time. Then FRANCINE exits.*

TANNER BRAEDEN: Beth—

BETH: Look, Tanner, just don't worry about all that old stuff. I forgive you. It's fine. Leave it where it belongs.

TANNER BRAEDEN: Does that have to be the end of the conversation?

BETH: Yes. Because it wasn't just the girls, remember, it was also the fighting.

TANNER BRAEDEN: We fought a lot. And it wasn't fun. / But we're mature now.

BETH: Fun?! No, it wasn't fun for me, because I never got to do any of the screaming. That was all you. You'd yell at me for everything, you'd blame me for everything, or you'd blame my friends or my family, there was always something wrong with me that pissed you off. Always.

TANNER BRAEDEN: I'm not that way anymore, ask anyone! Ask my friends, ask—you know, I have a lot of friends that are girls, ask them! I really learned from my mistakes. You did that. You changed me for the better.

BETH: And what about me?

Beat.

TANNER BRAEDEN: What about you?

BETH: You are such a narcissist. I'm just the collateral damage of your personal growth. As long as it made you a better person it was all worth it, right? How do you think you changed me?

TANNER BRAEDEN: You are so determined to make this not work, you've already decided I'm this bad person with bad intentions and what am I supposed to do with that? Is it my fault you're so fucking frigid?

BETH: Just fuck off.

TANNER BRAEDEN: Listen to me.

BETH: No.

TANNER BRAEDEN grabs her by the shoulders and shakes her.

TANNER BRAEDEN: You don't fucking listen. You don't. I don't know why you don't want me when I'm perfectly nice to you, I've always been nice to you, I've always listened to you and put up with your shit and that's not enough for you?

BETH: You're hurting me.

TANNER BRAEDEN: Good!

He lets go and takes a step back.

BETH: It's time for you to go now.

TANNER BRAEDEN: Beth, I'm so sorry. I'll go. I'm going. Call me later, please. Please.

TANNER BRAEDEN exits. CROW flies in.

CROW: That was wrong.

Beat.

He shouldn't have done that.

Beat.

It was bad.

BETH: *(snapping)* I know it was bad.

Beat.

Sorry. I know it was bad.

CROW: Why does he get to do that?

BETH: He's just like that sometimes. Sometimes he's not. He's just as capable of tenderness.

CROW: Though perhaps not as prone.

SCENE 8

Two days later. FRANCINE enters the backyard with JIM, who has a bunch of papers. She's nervous. Something's up.

FRANCINE: Beth, are you out here? Hi, Beth. Hi.

BETH: Hi.

FRANCINE: Beth, you remember Jim? He's here from the homeowners' association.

JIM: Hi.

BETH: Hi.

FRANCINE: He just wanted to ask you about the feeders.

JIM: Look, I'm just going to cut right to it. Beth, your crows are defecating everywhere. On my car, on my house—

BETH: The Audi or the Lexus?

FRANCINE: Beth!

JIM: Listen, it has to stop. Here's list of signatures from all the homeowners in the cul-de-sac asking you to stop.

He offers the papers. BETH *doesn't take them.*

BETH: Except my mom.

JIM: Well yes. But everyone else has had enough. Look at these feeders. They're huge. They're out of control. They're attracting all kinds of pests and rodents. People don't want to have rats in their houses just so you can feed a horde of defecating, screaming birds. It has to stop, today.

BETH: Thanks for coming by, Jim.

JIM: Listen to me, you have to stop. Why do the rest of us have to suffer? Look at all this food!

BETH: I'm not doing anything illegal.

JIM: I'm just asking you to consider your neighbours.

BETH: Okay.

JIM: Listen I can't have you—we can't have you, we the neighbourhood I mean, we can't have you attracting pests and birds. My house is covered!

BETH: It's my backyard.

JIM: We are a prized neighbourhood known for having nice houses.

BETH: Big houses. Beige with taupe / highlights. Suited to your taste.

FRANCINE: / Beth, don't—

JIM: Cut the bullshit, Beth. This is not your right. Property value is dropping. My car is covered in shit. Are you going to clean it?

BETH: Why not have the help take care of it?

JIM: Are you trying to insinuate I'm a bad person for having a house and car that I care about? You live here too, although I know you *(looks to FRANCINE)* inherited this place / and your house is the most shit-covered house on the block. I would think that you'd mind.

FRANCINE: / Look, I understand, Jim.

BETH: I don't mind shit. I'm putting up with a lot of it right now.

JIM: Cease and desist.

BETH: Birds shit, / Jim.

FRANCINE: / Okay, thanks for coming by, Jim. I'll take those.

JIM: Bullshit, Beth.

BETH: Anyone ever tell you, you catch more flies with honey than vinegar?

JIM: Get rid of them, or we're going to take it to the police.

BETH: Is that a threat? Are you threatening me? / Why don't you do something about it right now, Jim? Since you're the big man in charge?

FRANCINE: / That's really not necessary. / Jim, we'll scale it back a bit. I'm asking you to leave now, Jim.

JIM: The next time one of those fucking crows comes near my house, I'm going to fucking wring its neck and hang it from my goddamn balcony!

BETH: Try it, Jim!

FRANCINE: Everybody, that's enough. Jim, you'd better go.

JIM exits.

That's not—you can't talk to people that way, Beth, and expect to get what you want. I'm on your side.

BETH: But you want me to be sensible.

FRANCINE: You are sensible. I love you. You are extremely sensible. Just in your own way.

BETH: He can't stop us, can he? Legally?

FRANCINE: I don't know. There's damage, but it's not like his roof is caving in. Are they going to arrest every bird that poops on a car? I don't think so.

FRANCINE exits. CROW flies in.

CROW: Now what are you going to do about him.

BETH: I'll probably have to stop. Or at least pull back. Won't I? If he's getting the police involved.

CROW: I suppose. You're willing to give it all up for him.

BETH: No. Not for him. But for the good of the neighbourhood, I guess.

CROW: That's very selfless of you, to think of the other people. Very neighbourly. All the people living here must be just as selfless and thoughtful. How many of them are helping you get back on your feet?

BETH: What do you mean?

CROW: You're out of a job. Facing fines. How many of them are helping you?

BETH: None.

CROW: Oh. Well how many of them have offered help?

BETH: None.

CROW: How many have offered comforting words in this trying time?

BETH shakes her head.

I see. Well then you are very, very selfless indeed.

BETH: Okay, I get it.

SCENE 9

The CROW flies in and drops a dead baby bird on one of the feeders.

BETH: What is it?

CROW: A present, you know, a little something.

BETH: What?

CROW: I caught it or no—found it, and I could have it or I could give it to you and I wanted to give it to you. Beth, what's wrong?

BETH: I don't want a dead baby bird!

CROW: Why not?

BETH: Did you kill it?

CROW: What if I said yes, Beth? Or what if I said no? If I did kill it, would you hate me?

BETH: Stop it.

CROW: What if I told you this bird was evil? A murderer? Committing great injustices?

BETH: Did you kill it or didn't you?

CROW: What if it was hit by a car? What if it died of natural causes? Which death is the best death by your reckoning, Beth?

BETH: Tell me the truth!

CROW: There is violence and there is righteous violence and there is death and for you there is nothing similar between them. You don't have to be afraid, Beth! The bird is dead. The bird died. You prefer buttons and beads? What feeling is there in a gift like that? What I brought you is a gift for a strong girl. For a warrior girl. This is a gift for Joan of Arc.

BETH: I'm not Joan of Arc.

CROW: You could be, Beth. You just need a cause. And you could bear a shield. Armour with dead baby birds all over the chest plate, and you could burn on the pyre for your baby bird! Or maybe I didn't bring you a victim—maybe I brought you a villain and you could seek out the rest. You're capable, Beth. You have the spirit for it—that's why you can talk to me and that's why we're friends.

BETH: No. No. Stop it now! That is not friendship! That is not friendship! That is something else!

CROW: How would you know, Beth?

BETH: You have to be nice to me because you are a secret and if I told on you that would be the end of you and me and you would starve and you would die!

CROW: No Beth, listen to yourself. You are a secret. You're a secret pretending to be a woman.

BETH: What does that mean? What does that mean?

CROW: What happened at the Superstore?

SCENE 10

Flashback to STEPHEN's *office at the Superstore.*

STEPHEN: Thanks for coming in, Beth. I received your request for an increase in wages. Let's talk about that. You've been working here a year, and you've been getting your scheduled increases, but you're asking for this one a little early. Why?

BETH: Well, my department is down two people, including my supervisor. You haven't hired anyone to replace them, but we're expected to maintain productivity while taking on the supervisor responsibilities.

STEPHEN: Well I am very grateful for all your patience in that department. We're working on replacing the lost workers but it takes time.

BETH: I understand. In the meantime I think I should be fairly compensated for the work I'm doing. It doesn't make sense for me to do more work for the same wage. The duties I agreed to when I started have changed and so I think my wage should change too. I need to be making eighteen dollars an hour to make a living wage.

STEPHEN: I appreciate your concern and I understand your situation. Hell, we all have bills to pay, right?

BETH: Right now, I can't afford to pay them.

STEPHEN: I'm sorry but we just don't pay grocery clerks eighteen dollars an hour.

BETH: I'm not asking for eighteen dollars an hour, I'm asking for sixteen dollars.

STEPHEN: Well, considering your situation, I can see fit to raise your wage by fifty cents.

  Pause.

BETH: May I ask why you won't raise it by the full dollar I asked for?

STEPHEN: Let's pull out your recent performance reviews, shall we?

BETH: Okay.

STEPHEN: So the last one was conducted by Barry looks like, right?

BETH: Yeah, but he is actually the supervisor for another department. He doesn't actually work with me but after Geoff left he had to do that review since Geoff still hasn't been replaced.

STEPHEN: Looks like we have good scores here, you're on time, no no-shows, you get all your work done. However, Barry has some concerns about your customer service skills.

BETH: What concerns?

STEPHEN: You just don't go that extra mile when it comes to interacting with customers.

BETH: Have there been any complaints?

STEPHEN: No, not that. But you could go the extra mile. You know, smile more.

BETH: Barry thinks I should smile more?

STEPHEN: The approachability could use some work. It's the first impression that counts.

Pause.

BETH: What else does Barry think I should do?

STEPHEN: We have professional standards here, and you're just not meeting them. You know who you should talk to about this? Tara. She's known for being really approachable.

BETH: I can't be Tara.

STEPHEN: You could take a few pages from her book, couldn't you, in terms of professional appearance?

BETH: Is this because I don't wear makeup.

STEPHEN: I didn't say that. I said approachability. That's just one area you need to work on.

BETH: You don't wear makeup.

STEPHEN: *(laughs but not warmly)* I love your wit, Beth. That's what I like about you.

BETH: You want to shine me up like an apple.

STEPHEN: Calm down, Beth. That's not what I'm saying. Unfortunately, fifty cents is the best we can do right now until those professional areas improve.

BETH: I have bills I have to pay yesterday.

STEPHEN: Well, frankly Beth, you could find another job.

Beat.

Beth, this is not my problem.

BETH: But you're the one who controls—

STEPHEN: I don't think I'm getting through to you, Beth. There are a thousand other people who would kill to have a stable job like this.

BETH: You can't talk to me like that

STEPHEN: I think you should go back to work now, Beth, and try to calm down. I can get you in touch with an HR person who can refer you to some people who could help you with your anger.

BETH: You can't do that. Do you realize what you're doing to me? You can make my life so much easier by giving me this raise and you won't because of some bullshit excuse about professionalism and approachability. How do you sleep at night?

STEPHEN: I sleep just fine. Just fine. You know, I'm not sure how well you're really fitting in as part of the team here. Unfortunately, I'm going to have to write you up for talking to me like that, it's incredibly unprofessional, which is an emerging theme with you. If your attitude doesn't change soon / you'll find yourself out of work altogether. Yes, Beth, your attitude. Maybe it's just a cultural difference, I don't know how things work on the rez, but you can't speak to your superiors this way.

BETH: / My attitude? My attitude?

Why do you assume I lived on a rez? I never lived on a rez. I'm from here. I was born here. And I grew up here. My attitude. My attitude. You don't like me, and that's what it comes down to. You don't have to like me and you don't. I don't go out of my way to make you like me and so you don't like me. You want to fire me for that. You can fire me for that. You probably will.

STEPHEN: Alright Beth, you can finish your shift and then go home. You know, if you do find another job it will be difficult for me not to mention this interaction.

BETH: You're threatening me.

STEPHEN: Actions have consequences.

BETH: I asked for a raise. I asked for a raise. I asked for a raise. I asked for a raise and now you don't want me working here or anywhere else. I asked for a raise.

STEPHEN: Please leave my office now, Beth.

BETH: Are you fucking Tara, is that it?

STEPHEN: How dare you. How dare you. What did she say?

BETH: Oh my God, that is it. That's it isn't it. I asked for a raise.

STEPHEN: Get the fuck out of here, you're fired. You're done. You will never find another job if I can help it and you will die in squalor with the rest of your illiterate tax-dodging tribe, you fucking ugly dyke.

> *Screeching music.* BETH *gets up and leaves the office. She gets a knife and a steak. She impales* STEPHEN'S *office desk. She knocks over a pyramid of soup cans. She starts a fire in the magazines.*

BETH: I guess I was supposed to say thank you for the fifty cents and leave. I guess I was just supposed to get a better job. I guess I was supposed to file a complaint with my HR. I guess I was supposed to wait years for the union to take up my case. I guess I was supposed to empower myself with makeup. I guess I was supposed to be grateful to have a job at all. I guess I was supposed to keep my questions to myself. I guess I should have kept myself safe that way. I guess I was supposed to wait for the right time. I guess I was supposed to think of other people. I guess I was supposed to put myself second. I guess I was supposed to give a little more before I took. I guess I was supposed to hope that eventually my raise would come. I guess I was supposed to remember my boss is trying his best. I guess I was supposed to try my best. I guess I was supposed to try harder. I guess I was supposed to keep my feelings under control. I guess I was supposed to just go home and cry there. None of those seemed real. Those didn't seem like real options. I thought I'd rather die than do any of the things I was supposed to do. I felt like I was dying. I felt like I was sitting in that chair and dying. I was thinking about my unpaid bills and dying. I was thinking about my face and it felt dead. I was thinking and feeling until I felt like I was vibrating in my chair. I wondered how come he couldn't see that my whole body was vibrating. The chair was vibrating and the floor was vibrating. Can't anybody else feel the entire building vibrating? I felt like I was dead. I felt cold hard earth all around me. I felt dead. I felt like I was dead.

CROW: And then you felt real.

BETH: I felt really real. The knife felt real in my hand. The bloody steak looked so real on the desk. Barry's head felt real and my hands felt real. I felt like I was in control. I felt like I was working. I felt like I was doing something. I felt like I was real.

CROW: There is nothing wrong with that at all. At all. At all.

BETH: But I only made things worse for myself. How I am supposed to get a job now? How am I supposed to feed myself now? How am I supposed to make friends now? How am I supposed to feel real now?

CROW: I can show you. I'm sorry about the baby bird.

BETH: It's okay. It's not your fault. I felt real looking at that baby bird.

SCENE 11

Five days later in the early hours of the morning. The bird feeders have been destroyed. There are a few dead crows hanging from tree branches and the fence. CROW is around. BETH enters followed swiftly by FRANCINE.

BETH: I'm going to fucking kill somebody.

FRANCINE: / Oh my God. Oh my God. What happened?

BETH: I'm going to fucking kill somebody.

FRANCINE: / Oh, Beth, I'm so sorry.

BETH: Look what they did. Look what they did!

FRANCINE: / Beth, I'm so, so sorry. Oh God, how awful.

BETH: They killed them!

FRANCINE: No look, there's still some in the trees.

BETH: They hung dead crows from every single balcony in the cul-de-sac.

FRANCINE: I'm so sorry.

BETH: They took it from me! They want to take everything from me.

FRANCINE: It was probably just one person, don't you think?

BETH: No Mom, you aren't listening. You just aren't paying attention! They want to take everything from me! There's an evil that is working away at me and it wants me any way it can get me and it did this and it made them do this, and keep doing this, and it will keep doing this until there's nothing left of me and every time I stand up to it, it comes back harder and meaner than before, and every little bit of life I have it wants to absorb from me until there's nothing, nothing, nothing left of anything alive.

FRANCINE: I don't know who would do such a thing.

CROW: I do.

FRANCINE: What?

BETH: Mom, go inside.

FRANCINE: What?

BETH: Go inside, Mom. Please.

CROW: I know who did it.

FRANCINE: / Oh my God, oh my God, Beth. You—what?

BETH: Mom, please go now. If you're scared now, please go before it gets worse. Please go back inside.

FRANCINE exits.

CROW: I know who did it.

BETH: Tell me.

CROW: And I know what we're going to do about it.

BETH: Tell me everything.

CROW: Get your collection.

> *BETH goes and gets the tackle box that contains her collection of items from the CROW.*

BETH: Here it is.

CROW: Good.

BETH: Okay, what do we need.

CROW: All of them.

BETH: All?

CROW: All.

BETH: What are they for?

CROW: They're from the neighbourhood. All these items were found in your cul-de-sac.

BETH: This?

She pulls out a bead.

CROW: That belongs to house number forty-three. Courtney's necklace. She threw it out. I took the bead.

BETH: This?

She pulls out the wheel from a toy car.

CROW: House number twenty-seven. Anthony.

BETH: You little thief.

CROW: It's in my nature.

BETH: What do we do with these?

CROW: A lot. We can do a lot of things with these.

BETH: With magic?

CROW: Yes.

BETH: Cool.

CROW: I can show you. We just need a plan.

SCENE 12

TANNER BRAEDEN comes over—he thinks, to reconcile.

TANNER BRAEDEN: Hi Beth. How are you holding up?

BETH: Not great.

TANNER BRAEDEN: But you want to talk to me about it?

BETH: Yeah, I really feel I can confide in you.

TANNER BRAEDEN: Really?

BETH: No, not really, I hear you've been shooting birds.

TANNER BRAEDEN: Where did you hear that?

BETH: Around.

TANNER BRAEDEN: Did the crows tell you?

   Pause.

Look, of course I had nothing to do with this. It's awful. But I'm here to make you feel better. Look, I brought some more wine. I want to talk about, you know, it's a shame, Beth, we're getting along. I thought we were getting along.

BETH: We were.

TANNER BRAEDEN: I thought we were getting along like we used to.

BETH: We were not getting along like we used to.

TANNER BRAEDEN: Until the other day.

BETH: We were not getting along like we used to.

TANNER BRAEDEN: Why not? Why can't we?

BETH: You are a liar.

TANNER BRAEDEN: When? What was a lie?

BETH: Are you shooting crows?

TANNER BRAEDEN: No!

BETH: Did you do it?

TANNER BRAEDEN: Do what?

BETH: I know you are not half as adorably oblivious as you want me to think.

TANNER BRAEDEN: I don't get it. You asked me over here just so you could tell me that I'm a bad person for shooting at birds. So fucking what? We are overrun with birds in this neighbourhood and it is all your fault. Does it make you feel better? Do you like feeling like you're better than me? Does it make you feel like an angel? Watch this.

He takes the rifle and aims it at a bird in a tree. BETH *tries to grab the gun but he knocks her over.*

You can't stop me! I can do whatever I want!

He aims the gun at her.

I could hurt you right now! I could shoot you in the eye with this but I know the difference between shooting people and shooting at some dumb bird!

He lowers the gun.

BETH: Did you do it?

TANNER BRAEDEN: What are you gonna do? What are you gonna do, Beth?

BETH: Shoot me! Go ahead and shoot me!

He turns to leave. BETH *grabs a wine bottle, goes up behind him, grabs his arm and turns him around, knocks him over the head. He falls to the ground and drops the rifle. She picks it up and points it at him.*

Did you do it? Did you fucking do it? Did you do this? Did you shoot the birds and hang them on the balconies and scatter them in my backyard? Did you desecrate my bird feeders? Did you?

TANNER BRAEDEN: *Please don't shoot, please, Beth, Beth, I'm sorry, Beth, I'm so sorry, please don't shoot me, Beth I'm begging you!*

BETH: Yes you are! Finally! You've never been sorry for anything you've ever done—you're only ever sorry you got caught! You're still a little boy, you'll always be a little boy, because you will never have to grow up because you can just pretend you didn't know any better! You don't know when you are manipulating me so you couldn't really be manipulating me. You said before you know what I'm like. Did you know I'm like this?

TANNER BRAEDEN: Beth! It wasn't me. It wasn't me. I didn't do it. I swear to God.

BETH: Confess.

TANNER BRAEDEN: It was everybody. Everybody did it. Jim and some other guys from the neighbourhood came around and they had this big plan and they wanted everyone in the cul-de-sac to do it.

BETH: Is this supposed to absolve you? What kind of answer is this, everyone did it?

TANNER BRAEDEN: It wasn't my idea!

BETH: Of course not, this idea takes guts. But did you do it?

TANNER BRAEDEN: Not all of it. Not all of it!

She hits him with the butt of the rifle. He's unconscious. She drops it.

BETH: I can't do it.

CROW: Why not?

BETH: I keep hoping he can change. Like how I changed.

CROW: No he can't.

BETH: Well no, not like how I can change. But he can change as a person, as a human.

CROW: You trust him.

BETH: Yes he's cowardly. Yes. This we knew. I said he was like a little boy. I can't shoot a little boy.

TANNER BRAEDEN starts coming to.

CROW: He's just pretending. He could have changed when you were sixteen. He could have changed last week. He laid his hands on you. He participated.

BETH: I can't just shoot him in the head.

CROW: Neither can I.

TANNER BRAEDEN is getting up. He gets the rifle.

BETH: I know.

CROW: Alright.

BETH: What happens next?

TANNER BRAEDEN cocks the rifle. BETH turns around.

TANNER BRAEDEN: You're psychotic. I'm psychotic. Why is that bird talking?

BETH: He's my ally.

TANNER BRAEDEN: I can't listen to this. I can't listen to this. It's crazy.

Beat.

Explain yourself!

BETH: You just said you won't listen.

TANNER BRAEDEN: I'm pointing a loaded weapon at you. You struck me, Beth. Violently. If I shoot you—

BETH: It was self-defence, right? Protection, right? You were just protecting yourself from another violent halfbreed with a history of mental illness. You could shoot me with no consequences. The only hitch is I'm not on your property, otherwise you'd be acquitted no problem, but I think the wine bottle makes up for that, right?

CROW: Ask her why she's not frightened.

BETH: Ask me.

TANNER BRAEDEN: How are you doing that?

BETH: I'm not explaining myself to you anymore.

TANNER BRAEDEN: You were going to kill me.

CROW: That was the plan, anyway.

TANNER BRAEDEN: I have every right to defend myself.

Beat.

BETH: Well, go on.

He fires. Time slows down. BETH *turns into a crow. She flies at him and plucks his eyes out. She lands on some bird feeder remains.* CROW *picks him up and turns him into a mole. He drops* TANNER BRAEDEN *onto the ground.*

CROW: Good thing I came up with a Plan B.

SCENE 13

BETH, in human form, gets out her tackle box. She pulls out an empty key ring. She tosses it to CROW who catches it in his mouth.

BETH: Jim Abernathy!

JIM appears.

JIM: Wh—

BETH: Jim Abernathy! You are summoned here to answer for your crimes. How do you plead?

JIM: How is this happening? How the fuck is this happening?

BETH: Hey! Jim! How do you plead?

JIM: You made us do it.

BETH: Guilty then. I will now pass righteous judgment onto thee. Jim Abernathy, being sound of mind, able and willing, dedicated only to himself, did murder / and pillage, and wreak destruction contrary to the will of God, the heavens, and earth.

JIM: Wait a minute. Murder? Wait. Wait!

BETH: This is my show. Quiet!

JIM's mouth keeps moving but no sound comes out.

You don't feel you are culpable on these grounds: you weren't alone, and it was actually my fault for antagonizing you, am I correct?

JIM nods.

Very well. You feel you can hold me accountable for my actions, but you are not my father, my son, nor are you my Holy Ghost. You assumed a position and made sure it was powerful. But you failed to realize I am more qualified in this field than you are. I know all about actions and consequences. I know about being held accountable. Consequences are always propelled in my direction. I am made to suffer for my sins. I have suffered. I have pained. I have lost. I am penitent. I have been penitent. I have flagellated, and I have cursed myself, and I have been cast out. I have been exorcised. It's true. I did wrong. I dented our society. I dented it with my willful actions. By committing injustices, I have become fluent in the language, and I hear it in the mouths of everybody who would keep their boot on my neck to avoid a boot on theirs. Do you know what a polyglot is?

JIM shakes his head.

A polyglot is someone who can speak many languages. Like Crow.

CROW: Hello.

BETH: So you see, there's a lot more going on than you thought. But that's okay, right? You just didn't know. So it's not your fault. You're only responsible for what you were aware of. I have responsibilities too.

She pulls TANNER BRAEDEN, *the mole, out of her pocket.*

That's Tanner. I really wanted to forgive him for everything. For his part in the bird feeders and for killing all those crows, for letting it all happen, for not warning me about it, for fooling around on me all those years ago, for utterly, utterly disappointing me these last few weeks. This was the best I could do. He's safer now, from his own future actions. I protected him from that. But that could have been accomplished by killing him, and I didn't kill him. This way, he can give to this world more than he takes. And I'm going to turn you all into animals.

JIM starts fidgeting and protesting.

If you can't be happy living as a lark, or an otter, or a porcupine you've already lost what makes living worthwhile. You are born, you live, and you bear witness to the greatest miracle ever devised. That's the gift, for everyone. Life is real.

Connection is real. Beauty is real, and truth is possible. You are fortuitous, for can experience it all. And then you die. I just wish you a better death than the crows in this neighbourhood got, and in this life there are no guarantees.

She puts TANNER BRAEDEN *on the ground and he scampers off.*

Goodbye, Tanner. So, Jim Abernathy, you have plead guilty to the charges levelled against you, and that is wisdom. I know you did it. Your actions: You killed as many crows as you could over several days.

You hoarded them in your freezer, in your shed, wherever you could. You set a date. You organized the neighbours. You distributed dead crows. You had them hung. You all came to my backyard in the dead of night and destroyed my bird feeders, and went on another killing spree while you were feeling lusty. You slunk back to your den. You planned that. You executed that. You thought you could get away with that. Your motive: to frighten me. But I have been frightened so often, and I've had enough. Your sentence:

She turns him into a porcupine.

CROW: Case closed.

SCENE 14

Three weeks later.

JANE: Jane Lafontaine reporting to you this afternoon on the regular news station broadcast about a strange occurrence in one of the city's far-flung suburbs. I visited this cul-de-sac just over a month ago but the area is barely recognizable now, as you can see. Then, I spoke to a tragic, fragile grocery clerk and her eccentric recluse mother about their crow-keeping set-up. Now, I speak only to a tangled mess of branches and BMWs. Then, an active community bustling with concerned inhabitants. Now, a ghost town and barren wasteland. Four weeks ago, earlier reporting, by me, indicated that there were indeed people living here four weeks ago, but now that has all changed. It appears as though the inhabitants have disappeared without a trace and no indication that they will reappear. My sources tell me that it happened overnight and it was either divine intervention or a clerical error. No trace of the people living here has been found and there are no leads in the investigation. Police and scientists agree: they have no idea what's going on here. Hopefully one day we will figure all this out, but until then, I'm Jane Lafontaine.

SCENE 15

That evening. FRANCINE is sitting in the backyard, which is cleaned of debris, but looking more overgrown. BETH enters with CROW.

BETH: I thought I was the one who was supposed to sit out here.

FRANCINE: I'm waiting for you.

BETH: I'm sorry about everything that happened here. I'm sure it hurt you. If you want to be far away from me I understand, and you can leave at any time. I get why raising me is so hard. I don't take well to direction. But I hope I was a good daughter sometimes, and that if that's the only way you want to know me, you don't have to stay here.

FRANCINE: I'm the one that got you the bird feeders in the first place. In for a penny, in for a pound.

BETH: They will be back, Mom.

CROW: They will.

FRANCINE: People die all the time. Your father did. And I wasted a lot of time then beating my breast and asking why. And how could this happen. And most importantly how could this happen to me. Trying to figure it all out. But there is never, and will never be, one answer for why things happen. We participate in life, certainly, but we only recognize if we've made the right decision after we've already made it, when we see what happens next. I want to see what happens next for you. So take me with you.

BETH: I'm not leaving.

FRANCINE: You can't stay here, can you, with me, being as spectacular and magical as you are. Not forever. That crow wasn't always here. He came here. From somewhere else. And from somewhere else before that. He's a travelling spirit like you.

BETH: I love you, Mom. I really love you. I can't even understand how much I love you.

FRANCINE: I love you too. And I will always be with you. I can always help you.

BETH: And I will always help you.

CROW: Don't worry because you are both more or less good people which is all you can really ask for. A normal life is full of mistakes. And sometimes you act like an asshole. And sometimes you deliberately cause harm. But other times you act on behalf of the meek. Which is good. I snuck into a church and saw a painting of a saint. It's good to have aspirations. Better to have aspirations that come with a suit of armour. Let's go.

> *FRANCINE and BETH turn into crows and fly off with CROW into the night.*

ACKNOWLEDGEMENTS

I need to begin by acknowledging the work of my extraordinary brother and co-founder of Thumbs Up Good Work Theatre, Colin Wolf. We started the company together in 2012, when I was twenty-two and he was twenty, with a Fringe Festival run of a show we wrote together called *Grow Up*, and we have been producing our work ever since. Colin has always been a huge source of inspiration and get-at-it-ness in my life. He encouraged me to write my first grant, to apply for playwrights units and theatre jobs, and we've just always been doing theatre ever since we were kids. I can't thank him enough for not just believing in me, but for being there alongside me, in the play, writing grants, cutting wood, finding venues, and so many countless other things. For doing it all the hard way and coming out the other side feeling so proud. Love you and I can't wait to see what you do next.

I also want to thank his wife and my sister-in-law, Sydney Wolf for all their tireless work on the set and props for this show—I can't imagine many people's first props gig involved porcupines, a raw steak, crows, and complicated fish-wire/pop-can target-practice set-ups. Thank you for taking that on and for making that vision a reality.

Thank you to Bryn, one of the most beautiful, loving, thoughtful people I have ever met. A true friend who is always there for me during hard times, and who introduced me to birding. I am so proud of you.

To Elena Belyea, who I am honoured to have known since we were in undergrad at the U of A, a million love yous and smooches on the top of your head. Your dramaturgy work on this script was such a gift, and so invaluable to the story, you are such a talent and I love that we are still in Alberta together. Say hi to Geoff and Bodie!

Huge thanks to the entire production teams for Thumbs Up Good Work Theatre for their hard work on this project.

Eternal gratitude to my family, my late mom, my dad, my in-laws Line and Rick, my Auntie Cindy, and Auntie Carol for their support. Can't say much more without getting choked up. We have gone through so much together this year. I couldn't have done this without you, I love you all so much.

I want to acknowledge the people who aren't here—my mom, Danielle, and my Grandma and Grandpa B.

And last but certainly not least, I have to acknowledge Sacha Crow in his capacity as my true love and life partner. Life gets better every day with you, I love you more every day. We've been hit hard, really hard, and at a younger age than most. I'd say we're gonna win the lottery one day but I already did, so we'll see if lightning strikes twice. Thank you for your acceptance of your curmudgeonly stepson, Frank, our beautiful little jade-eyed Bill, and of course, the real star of the show, Senor.

Caleigh Crow is a queer Metis theatre artist from northeast Calgary. Previous playwriting topics include a talking crow and a grocery clerk, the mass coronal ejection of 1859, the Antifa supersoldier, the intersection between twelfth century Franciscan nuns and Britney Spears, remote viewing, witch revenge, and a landlord musical. She is the co-founder and artistic lead of Thumbs Up Good Work Theatre. Her work tends towards themes of metaphysics, class struggle, magic, and serious whimsy.